Lusaka to London in ANA45

Tales from along the way

by

Robert Walker

Grosvenor House
Publishing Limited

This book is published by
Grosvenor House Publishing Ltd
Link House
140 The Broadway, Tolworth, Surrey, KT6 7HT.
www.grosvenorhousepublishing.co.uk

A CIP record for this book
is available from the British Library

ISBN 978-1-80381-739-2

Dedication

This short account of various incidents which took place during my overland travels from Lusaka to London in 1986 is dedicated to my beautiful granddaughter Niamh. May she use her amazing and fearless spirit to conquer all life's challenges and forge her own unique path.

March 2023

Acknowledgements

This collection of some of the many incidents along the way would never have happened if I'd flown home in February 1986 from Zambia instead of going overland by Land Rover. That I was able to undertake this journey in the first place was due to my now ex-wife's selfless commitment to look after our two small children on her own whilst I fulfilled my dream. Thank you Vanessa.

To Melanie on that flight from George to Capetown in 2022, your genuine and spontaneous encouragement spurred me into action after 36 years!

To Paul Golson, Jeff Bond and Mr Banda the welder from Lewis Construction, a heartfelt thanks for your support in preparing the vehicle. Paul, if you weren't aware before, you are now!

To Mike Mallaghan, my dear friend in Lusaka where I stayed in 2023 and who gave me the time and space to get the majority of this onto my laptop. Thank you for putting up with me Mike!

To my friend James (name changed) at the British High Commission in Lusaka. You're retired now I think. Thanks for getting Peter home!

To the Eastern European doctors along the way who insisted on giving me a vaccination against meningitis, thanks!

To the English couple who sold me their roof rack, thank you!

To all the great fellow overlanders out there, keep on overlanding!

Prologue

25th November 2022

"You should write the book" said Melanie, the lady sitting next to me on Flight 4Z622 from George in South Africa to Cape Town.

She'd boarded almost last and we were seated in the row with the emergency exit doors over the wings and had extra leg room as a result. Clearly we were both seasoned air travellers!

Melanie was clutching a red plastic container on her lap, reminiscent of a school child's lunchbox. Jokingly I'd commented "So you've brought your own biscuits with you for the flight then"! Surprisingly I was correct. The box contained her mother's homemade shortbread, legendary as all mothers' baking is. I declined, my waistline and cardiologist said no!

We had chatted as you do during the short flight and I had learned that Melanie was South African, married to a fellow South African, educated in Singapore and currently living in San Francisco. Working in the tech industry she belonged to the young modern workforce that could work from pretty much any location with an internet connection. Her husband worked in construction, specialising in converting heritage buildings into modern work environments. These special buildings were owned by Global Tech Companies, where form and function fed creative minds in our modern technological world.

I describe their jobs and backgrounds because as someone who'd struggled with a fax machine in the past, I valued her opinion and reaction to my past analogue experiences.

"What brings you to South Africa" she'd asked? I'd shared with her how my original love affair with Africa was born in the 1980's.

I had been recruited through the British Government's Overseas Development Administration (ODA) as it was known in those days and was to be a lecturer in Hotel Management at the Evelyn Hone College in Lusaka, Zambia on a 2 year contract. I'd arrived as an enthusiastic and naive 26 year old single man. Those 2 years passed in a whirl, contracts were extended and subsequently renewed, and it wasn't until 6 years later, now married with 2 young children, that it was finally time to leave that beautiful country and return to England.

I had nurtured the dream of driving home across the continent in my ancient Land Rover and the ODA had agreed to fund me to the equivalent cost of my airfare. This would make the trip financially viable.

My wife and children flew home and less than 24 hours after saying goodbye they were back in our family home in Sevenoaks, Kent. My overland journey was slightly longer, 6 months in total.

I'd briefly recounted to Melanie the story of this and had touched on a couple of the experiences I'd had along the way.

As we taxied to the terminal at the end of the flight Melanie had said "You should write the book".

And so, some 36 years after making the overland trip, I did!

1980-1986

These were the 1980's in Zambia, independence in neighbouring Zimbabwe had just been declared. Supplies of essential commodities were erratic and unpredictable. Obtaining the local Mosi beer and cooking oil depended on who you knew rather than your ability to pay. The country suffered from poor infrastructure and in those days there were no mobile phones or sat navs to help route planning.

President Kenneth Kaunda (affectionately known as KK), was in his 17th year of office. I'd organised my UK wedding from Zambia by Telex from what was then the Ridgeway Hotel in Lusaka. Those houses lucky enough to own a landline phone had to book international calls hours in advance.

Against this background of shortages and communication challenges there was a wonderful generosity extended by locals, especially in rural areas, and fellow expats were hugely supportive.

Preparations for the epic (well epic in my mind at least) journey had taken 6 years. They included purchasing the Land Rover, a 109 series 3 station wagon and slowly replacing all the bits that had dropped off or stopped working. I'd also been gradually acquiring the essential overland kit (roof rack, jerry cans, tools etc.) from fellow overland travellers who had driven from England to Zambia and were selling off their possessions before flying home.

Finally my preparations were complete. The local construction firm had sponsored me, (largely unknown to the boss)! I had their logo on the side of the vehicle, a huge roof rack weighed down with 8 jerry cans and a roof tent, and a 300 litre locally built petrol tank located just behind the front seats. As a smoker in those

1

days, my journey, on reflection, could so easily have been rocket propelled with one careless toss of a cigarette end!

Farewells completed, every jerry can filled along with the two fuel tanks, I left Lusaka in February 1986. My travelling companion was a young Brit called Peter. My wife had insisted that I was accompanied on the journey. If I fell ill on the way there would be someone to summon help (how I wasn't quite sure as this was the pre mobile phone era). In any case it was safer than travelling alone. I had visions of a blonde female Scandinavian, naturally attractive and also a great cook. No mechanical knowledge required! My wife had other ideas. We'd advertised in the Times of Zambia for someone who wanted a free ride to the UK. Peter was the only applicant so of course he passed the selection interview by default! He met all the requisites, young, strong, a fellow Brit. What could possibly go wrong? It wouldn't take long for this question to be answered.

Departure Day 11th February 1986.

2

The Bullseye

Malaria was a common hazard in Zambia and throughout sub-Saharan Africa. I'd been struck down twice by it during my 6 year stay and was concerned about the implications of a third bout on my journey, miles from medical facilities.

My good friend Liam was a doctor in Lusaka and assured me all would be OK. He liberated from his surgery a supply of Chloroquine in glass phials along with several sterile needles and presented them to me. *"What am I supposed to do with those?"* I'd asked. *"You inject yourself if you suspect you've caught malaria and are unable to get medical help"* he replied. Now, I happen to have a pathological fear of needles, I'm sure there's a term for this condition, prickphobia, needleitis, I haven't researched this. My natural response when an injection was imminent was to tense up, stop breathing and look away whilst the nurse administered a dose of some vaccine. *"I can't do that"* I nervously told him. *"Look"* he said, *"I'll draw a circle in indelible ink on one of your buttocks and anywhere in the circle is good to aim for"*! That circle lasted for many weeks; thankfully I never needed to aim for that bullseye!

The First Breakdown

Day one of our journey and about eighty miles north of Lusaka, we stopped at a police roadblock. Contrary to some peoples' experience with African roadblocks, our experience was positive; the officers were polite and merely doing their job. One even helpfully pointed to an oil slick developing underneath the Land Rover whilst we were stationary. On closer inspection this seemed to be coming from the gearbox area. To my alarm, it looked as though the rear main engine oil seal had failed. The fact that we were severely overloaded hadn't helped here. My plan to spend all my remaining local currency (Zambian Zwacha) on petrol just before crossing the border out of Zambia was set to fail. That money would now have to be spent on a major garage bill.

Worryingly, a strange and rather unpleasant smell had also developed in the rear of the vehicle. I wondered if the two incidents were in some way connected. Peter seemed concerned at this latest development. The smell turned out to be a whole beef fillet which he'd acquired in Lusaka from some local butchery. As we had no fridge on board the inevitable was happening, a case study in bacterial decay.

In truth, I was more concerned with the practicalities of keeping the vehicle going rather than missing out on a Chateaubriand supper. A new oil seal had to be fitted otherwise sooner or later serious damage would occur. This meant removing the gearbox, a task that I wasn't able to do on the side of the road. As Peter was more interested in saving his beef fillet than assisting with vehicle repairs, we needed to find a garage, which we did in Kabwe.

Two days later repairs were complete and my reserves of local currency were gone. The huge additional fuel tank was no longer required, but was now taking up valuable space inside the Land Rover.

We continued on our journey eventually reaching Mbala, the border post with Tanzania. My Zambian Kwacha was now all gone. Paperwork was duly completed. The Carnet de Passage was stamped along with my passport and I'd handed in my Zambian ID card. Surprisingly I was sad to see it go. I'd been resistant to the idea originally of being required to carry identification at all times, yet after 6 years living in Zambia it seemed a sensible thing to do. I would have liked to have kept it as a memento but regulations meant it had to be surrendered on final exit.

Years later back in England I bumped into one of my old friends from Lusaka. I was mortified to learn that within hours of my unplanned breakdown word was all around Lusaka that Robert had only managed to travel 80 miles before breaking down! The news, spread by bush telegraph, had caused much merriment and comment at the time apparently. Toyota Land Cruiser owners shook their heads in despair! Thankfully at the time I'd no idea of the damage done to my reputation as an intrepid overlander!

After only 80 miles the gearbox is out.

ANA45

ANA45 was my Land Rover's number plate. I was hoping to retain this on my return to UK but sadly this would prove to be impossible.

This vehicle registration was always the source of merriment as we drove through the dusty potholed roads from Lusaka north to the border with Tanzania. Locals walking along the roadside would wave happily and smile, naturally cheerful in spite of difficult living conditions.

One day I discovered the reason why my vehicle caused amusement with some onlookers. Chatting with a young man he'd jokingly remarked *"So you are very strong Bwana"*! I knew I wasn't (hence the requirement for a travelling companion), so I replied *"but why do you say that my friend"? "But you have 45 children, Ah but you are just too strong"!*

By this point in the conversation I was somewhat bemused. *"You have 45 children"* he repeated, explaining that in the local language ANA meant children. Having many children was both a sign of virility, wealth and also an insurance against an uncertain future. I'm not sure how impressed he'd have been to find out that I 'only' had two children and certainly no wealth!

To this day I treasure these number plates, proudly displayed in my garage in Kent. They remind me of happy African days and even now, some 36 years later, my email address robtana45@live.co.uk incorporates ANA45!

Up Lake Tanganyika

At the southernmost point of Lake Tanganyika at Mpulungu the Land Rover was craned aboard the ferry MV Liemba and unceremoniously dumped on the deck. The next six hundred kilometres of our trip would be on water all the way up to Kigoma in Tanzania, a short distance then by road into neighbouring Burundi.

The ship was surrounded by vendors in smaller vessels loaded with fast food; nuts, bananas and so on which the many locals travelling on board bought for the 3 day journey. We were two white travellers amongst several hundred local foot passengers. At night I'd sleep in my roof tent, Peter inside the Land Rover. Little did I know what disruption lay ahead.

The next day dawned sunny and the temperature soon rose. Peter thought a swim was in order to cool off. Having climbed onto the roof of the Land Rover, before I could intervene, he had dived off into the murky waters below. An impressive dive but the ferry captain was less impressed. We were travelling slowly but too fast for Peter to catch up. The captain had no choice but to perform a sweeping U turn to rescue him. This incident I'm sure merely confirmed the locals' view of these two muzungus on board. Fortunately the goodwill prevailed and surprisingly we were allowed to continue our journey with no recriminations. Nor was I charged for the obvious inconvenience, extra fuel consumed and so on, such was the generosity we encountered.

After this unfortunate event we kept a low profile for the remainder of the journey on the lake, and arrived at Kigoma without further incident.

Aboard the MV Liemba.

Fast Food on Lake Tanganyika.

The Shaved Head

You don't see many travellers with shaved heads in hot climates. When you do they're generally wearing a head covering, bandana, cap or other form of headwear. The African sun can be relentless and sunstroke and dehydration are ever present risks to be mitigated. Having a full head of hair meant that I've always been reluctant to wear a hat!

Another characteristic of overlanders in those days was that they generally looked just like overland travellers! Their clothes reflected this fact. They wore bright coloured shirts, leather sandals, with fitted shorts for the more fashion conscious!

Vehicles too tended to adopt a similar appearance, tending to be white or solid plain colours, greens, blues even reds. Colours favoured by the military (such as sand or camo) tended to be avoided, as travellers who looked like insurgents ran a higher risk of being confronted. In an extreme case this might get you shot at should you be in the wrong place at the wrong time! Military action was certainly evident in Chad, and Nigeria had only just reopened its eastern border.

Shortly after the diving incident in Lake Tanganyika, Peter shaved his head. Being young and slim he could now quite easily be mistaken as a mercenary. I kept my counsel, after all he was entitled to dress and style his hair (or lack of now) as he pleased. This proved to be the start of his undoing.

The Silverback Gorillas

Days passed, we drove into Rwanda via Burundi. I'd heard about an area where if you were lucky you could find the famous mountain gorillas. I longed to see a Silverback, the mature males of the family, but poaching and pressures on their environment in the 1980s meant it wasn't easy to find them in the Virunga mountains.

A guide was recruited and we set off into the dense forest. After an hour or so the guide signalled for silence and there in a small clearing was a family group. A huge silverback who I assumed was the dominant male eyed us carefully but then thankfully carried on eating. It was truly a magnificent sight to watch such beautiful creatures in their natural habitat.

A Lowland Gorilla.

The Laundry Incident

More time passed, small pontoons were negotiated, border crossings endured, with much form filling and exchange of gifts in the form of Peter Stuyvesant cigarettes to speed up the process.

We were now in Zaire (renamed the Democratic Republic of Congo in 1997), one of the poorest and the second largest country in Africa. With appalling roads which were all but impassable during the rainy season, we faced a journey of over 2000kms, from Goma in the east to Bangui in the Central African Republic to the west. Torrential rain would be followed by clear blue skies and intense heat, making for an interesting sleeping experience as my roof tent leaked almost as much as the Land Rover.

Being young and away from polite society for several weeks, clothes washing hadn't figured large in the overall scheme of things. My normal dress was a fetching pair of black and orange shorts, flip flops and a T shirt for when the temperature dropped too much. Evenings could be cold, especially further north, and would even dip below freezing at night in the Sahara.

Our route took us via Kisangani on the banks of the mighty Congo river. With an overall length of nearly 5000kms, it's the second longest river in Africa, behind the Nile.

By the time I'd reached Zaire the issue of clean clothes had to be addressed. Parked up by the Congo where it was wide and slow moving, I took a lead from the locals, found a bar of soap and set to. Some considerable time later my collection of travelling clothes had been rubbed, scrubbed, rinsed, flogged and wrung out, an exhausting process for me in the heat. Laid out in the sun to dry, I was pleased with my efforts.

Time passed. I might have had a warm beer or several. An afternoon nap seemed in order. Waking up I realised I'd slept longer than I'd intended. I'd mapped out a suitable place to stop overnight away from towns and civilisation, as most nights were spent wild camping. If we were to arrive before dark we had to leave immediately. Some hours later we arrived, set up camp and ate. I thought how nice it would be to have clean clothes in the morning.

The next day I opened my small clothes locker, in the rear of the vehicle. It was empty. In despair I realised all my clothes except the ones I was currently wearing had been left on the banks of the Congo river, several hours drive away! No point in going back for them, by now they would have been rehomed.

I had learned a valuable lesson; don't wash clothes on a trip like this!

A Typical Road in Zaire.

A Good Bridge in Zaire.

14

Football Fever

It was now sometime in March 1986, and we were about to enter Cameroon from Chad at N'Djamena. The FIFA World Cup was to start in May but from memory Cameroon failed to qualify. As with any national event expectations were running high and there was a general excitement among the locals whenever their national side were playing.

The border post was low key, with rather dilapidated buildings, but I'd prepared accordingly. I'd changed into my one remaining 'smart' shirt, worn long to cover by now my extremely tatty and less fetching orange and black shorts. Flip flops dusted, hair brushed, I was ready for the usual excitement of another African border crossing.

As I did before each border crossing, I asked Peter to assure me that we were not carrying any illegal substances stashed in hidey-holes around the vehicle. As usual, he assured me that this was the case, no contraband was on board. I was never 100% sure that this was the case but short of dismantling the vehicle I had to take him at his word.

Passports ready, carnet to hand, cash in hand for any unexpected expenses including visas, I felt we were as prepared as we could be for this border. I was wrong!

My planning had failed to take into account that Cameroon was that day playing another African country, possibly Egypt, in the finals of the Africa Nations Cup. Supporters of these two teams would be glued to the one available black and white TV set available in their village or local bar, consuming vast quantities of the local beer (well certainly in Cameroon, I'm not sure about Egyptian drinking habits) made from whatever food staple was available. In Zambia this was maize, and the resulting off-white liquid was called chibuku, generally brewed in an old oil drum, tasting to my western palate as being virtually undrinkable. A mixture of something between paraffin and old bathwater.

The results were undeniable, loud singing and dancing, until a near comatose state of being was achieved.

On approaching the border post it was obvious that nobody was entering or exiting Cameroon today. Doors were closed, shutters down, no officials were to be found anywhere within sight of the border post. I spoke to a local who was patiently waiting; he was clearly not a football fan. He informed me that the customs and immigration staff were all watching the game at a nearby site which had a TV. I could only hope that Cameroon won the game, thus smoothing our border crossing. Unfortunately as we found out later they lost on penalties!

In-House Publishing

I'm not sure what it was about Chad that encouraged travellers to tow large trailers. Something in the air maybe.

Eric was a large chap with red cheeks and a full beard. I assumed he was South African but this wasn't confirmed. We'd met on the road as fellow travellers do and I'd been admiring his transport, a large Unimog truck, to my mind the king of all off road overland vehicles. These German Daimler-Benz trucks were immensely capable vehicles, if somewhat thirsty!

Behind this impressive machine was an enormous box trailer with a roller shutter entrance which Eric proudly opened to reveal the contents within. I must admit that I wasn't prepared for what I saw in front of me. It looked like an office complete with tables and chairs, photocopiers, printing machine, ink stamps, printing paper and so on. It could have been a small print works, complete with its own generator for power. In fact this is exactly what it was. I naively asked Eric if he ran a business with all this equipment. He looked at me carefully, I think he was deciding whether he could trust me, and proceeded to explain the purpose of this equipment.

In those days border crossings mainly revolved around manual systems to control immigration and customs. Computers were in their infancy and border post officials relied on form filling, official stamps, visas, letters of recommendation, invitation and so on. Getting visas could be a laborious process, sometimes involving the applicant leaving one country to fly to either their country of domicile to officially apply, or to the nearest regional embassy which issued these visas.

Eric was clearly a resourceful chap. He explained that if an official passport stamp or visa was required, he simply made his own, using his extensive array of equipment and obvious knowledge of the documentation required.

I decided it was better to ask no more questions and after a warm beer together we parted company.

The Swiss Couple

We were now in Chad and my initial impressions of this country hadn't been favourable. Military activity seemed intense. The French Foreign Legion was much in evidence. To the North there was conflict with Libya. I wasn't sure exactly what was happening where we were further to the South, yet I was keen to leave as soon as possible. I was aware that there was a military dictatorship in Nigeria where we were headed, so the prospects for the next couple of weeks weren't particularly positive!

I decided that wild camping wasn't safe and more by luck than judgement came across a walled area in the desert which served as a respite point for weary travellers. Facilities were basic but there was a feeling of security here together with other overlanders.

One afternoon as I sat in my battered chair surveying the harsh scenery, I noticed in the distance a small cloud of dust heading towards the camp. This grew steadily larger and I could make out the distant outline of two vehicles. The one in front was pulling a large box trailer. I remember thinking at the time that this seemed inappropriate given the road conditions.

A few minutes later the two vehicles pulled into the camp. A young European lady jumped out of the first vehicle, and as I was about to learn, her husband alighted from the following vehicle. Warm beers were exchanged and drunk and we chatted as travellers do. I found out that they were from Switzerland, both professionals with excellent jobs and career prospects. Naturally I asked why they were travelling with two vehicles and also towing the large trailer. Surely this was an inefficient way to travel? Towing would slow progress and cause major challenges during the rainy seasons they would encounter along the way. Roads further south would become bogged and were frequently impassable.

They explained their situation to me. As well paid professionals in their home country they had acquired the usual trappings of success. These included a nice house, furniture and a comfortable standard of living. However what they felt they lacked was freedom. I wasn't totally sure what they meant by this but apparently they felt the requirements to fit in socially were too restrictive. This might for example be the requirement not to cut your lawn on a Sunday or use power tools after a certain time, I fail to recall the exact examples they gave.

These restrictions were sufficient however to cause them to sell up all but their most treasured belongings. These remaining possessions filled the trailer. The plan was to drive around the world until they found their personal paradise. Then they would settle down.

I was left feeling humbled by their sense of genuine adventure. My efforts were little in comparison. I had a house in UK, a wife and two children to return to. I had made little sacrifice to set off on my adventure. In reality my wife was the one who was making the sacrifice, caring for two very young children on her own so I could live my dream.

As the Swiss couple left the next day in a cloud of dust I remember wishing them good luck in finding their paradise. Yet somehow I suspected that for them it was as much about the journey itself as it was about the destination!

Sickness on Board

Whilst we often encountered the most beautiful scenery on route, the reality was that overland travel involved hours of noisy and bone shaking vibrations from the appalling roads. Deep corrugations on gravel roads shook every nut and bolt to destruction. Shock absorbers gave up working above a certain speed, unable to keep up with the continuous up and down motion which generated huge amounts of heat and frequently resulted in components failing.

The Land Rover was by now showing its age. The engine rasped, the gearbox and drive train continuously whined, the old cart springs creaked and groaned and subsequently broke completely. The roof rack, severely overloaded, tried to go in the opposite direction to the vehicle when cornering. Essentially it was travel at a most basic level.

Being young and optimistic however, this didn't worry me particularly. This was freedom, 4x4 travel meant I could go anywhere (well almost anywhere), and the ambient noise was all part of the experience.

In this noisy environment conversation was difficult as you couldn't realistically hear what your passenger was saying! Peter had spent several hours trying to explain chaos theory to me without success. I simply couldn't understand how a leaf falling in Venezuela might cause a flood in Pakistan. We had little in common and gradually over the miles, he'd given up speaking to me entirely; probably judging that being married with two children I had different priorities and was a lost cause.

After several days without conversation it became apparent that it wasn't just a clash of personality that was responsible for the silence.

Peter was now slumped in the passenger seat, pale and sweating, definitely unwell. I suspected he had sunstroke at the very least. His shaven head and lack of headgear hadn't helped here.

As the situation dramatically unfolded, my diagnosis would turn out to be correct but nowhere near complete. Things would eventually get much more serious.

The Next Breakdown

We were now in Algeria, driving through a desolate featureless sandscape. It was searingly hot and we were miles from anywhere. Making progress was difficult, the tracks were unpaved and in poor condition. I struggled on as fast as I dared; the old Land Rover springs were taking a battering.

From In Guezzam our route took us to Tamanrasset and then on to Assakrem, high in the Hoggar mountains. Experiencing sunrise over the Hoggar was one of those experiences not to be missed and I was looking forward to this,

Suddenly, the moment that every overland driver hopes never to experience; there was a huge explosion from under the vehicle's bonnet, followed by clouds of steam. I could even see pieces of splintered metal flying randomly from the front of the Land Rover. We came to an abrupt halt; we were effectively going nowhere.

It didn't take long to establish what had happened. On lifting the bonnet the damage was obvious. The radiator was holed and beyond repair. The heavy duty military fan which I'd smuggled back from the UK in my hand luggage on a Zambia Airways flight had indeed proved its rigidity. It was so strong and heavy that it had caused the water pump bearing to fail. When the pump subsequently seized the fan had flown off straight through the radiator. Prognosis, complete disaster! I had a spare water pump bearing on board but no spare radiator or fan. We were in the middle of nowhere, no AA, very little passing traffic, and with insufficient spares to repair or do even a temporary fix. My passenger needed urgent medical assistance and now we were stationary.

I knew from my research into overland travel in hostile environments that you should stay with the vehicle and make SOS signs from whatever was to hand. With luck these might be seen by a passing aircraft. Attempts to walk out to seek help could at best end in either dehydration from the relentless Saharan sun or hypothermia from the freezing night temperatures. Unless you knew the area and likely points of human contact walking out would probably end badly.

I slept fitfully that night. Peter was still slumped in the passenger seat but not obviously worse. Hours passed, the sun finally rose and with it so did the temperature. I started to work removing all the damaged parts. These were soon disassembled and unceremoniously laid out in a heap on the dusty ground. The effort felt good. I was doing something positive to resolve the situation. In truth though, with no replacement parts, unless a miracle happened, we were likely to spend days, maybe even weeks stranded there.

Then amazingly, the wonderful sound of a labouring engine. A young Dutch couple in a 4x4 came into view.

There was no need to flag them down, our situation was obvious. The raised bonnet of the Land Rover and pile of broken parts clearly told the story. Help was at hand! Toyota drivers may not be aware of this wonderful feeling of relief as their vehicles of course just don't break down!

We exchanged stories and they agreed to take me to back to Tamanrasset where I would try to find some spare parts for my vehicle. Peter was to remain with the vehicle; he had plenty of water and food if he felt able to consume either. On reflection I don't know why he didn't go with the Dutch couple as he needed medical help. There must have been a good reason but all these years later I can't recall what it might have been.

We set off and several hours later we arrived back in Tamanrasset where I was left to meet the locals. Word soon spread about my breakdown and a young man appeared and summoned me to his hut. His name was Ahmed and I explained to him what had happened and my need for spares, never for one moment expecting him to produce the necessary parts. Amazingly he had an old Land Rover and agreed that I could remove the fan and water pump from this and use them on my vehicle. Even more incredibly he produced a brand new radiator, still in its original Land Rover packaging, which he'd been intending to fit to his vehicle. It was for an earlier model than mine but I knew I could make it fit.

We discussed the issue of price, how much did he want for these valuable parts? We agreed that when I'd got my vehicle running again I'd return and he would have the pick of the many other Land Rover spares I had on board by way of payment. The possibility that I wouldn't return never crossed our minds, such was the bond which was created when people in need come together.

I set to and removed Ahmed's water pump and fan. Time has erased my memory of how I got back with these parts to Peter and my vehicle, several hours away. Quite possibly the Dutch couple had waited and taken me back, I cannot recall.

I quickly fitted the spares I'd brought back with me and several hours later nervously set off back to Tamanrasset. I stopped frequently to check that my modifications to the radiator pipework were holding up. All seemed to be working well. When we eventually arrived I set to and removed the water pump and refitted it to Ahmed's vehicle. I repaired my water pump with a new bearing and straightened out the blades on my fan as best as I could. I realised that another fan would be required as soon as I could find one as vibrations from the unbalanced fan would quickly ruin the new bearing I'd fitted.

With final adjustments made the time had come to settle up with Ahmed. I unpacked all my spares and he chose several small items along with my pride and joy, a brand new OE distributor, complete with HT leads. This had cost me dear in Lusaka as spares were extremely difficult to come by and very expensive when they were available. This was due to the lack of foreign exchange, hence imported goods were few and far between.

In truth, I was disappointed that Ahmed had chosen this as my current distributor was ancient and might well cause problems along the remaining journey to England. When I thought about his unfailing generosity however, I handed it over willingly and we parted as friends.

Once again I did not anticipate the results of this transaction. Maybe there was something to this chaos theory after all!

Breakdown on the way to Assakrem in Hoggar.

We were now able to resume our journey to Assakrem, arriving well after dark having negotiated some fearsome inclines on the climb up the plateau, over 8000 feet above sea level. It was extremely cold and we were exhausted after the breakdown. Amazingly there was a makeshift hostel at the top serving hot spaghetti, the most wonderful culinary experience!

Next morning we rose early and climbed to the summit to see the spectacular sunrise. My diary records: *'Up at 530, very blowy and cold (UK type of cold) Very steep walk up the hill to the top...quite a beautiful sight. Porridge to warm up, sold 5 Jerry cans then off at 830.'*

I imagine that I had no use for the jerry cans now and needed funds!

The road to Assakrem.

Medical Assistance

I'd realised that by now Peter was severely dehydrated, unable to take fluid, and I contemplated the worst if he didn't receive medical attention soon. I also discovered that somewhere between the border with Niger and our current location, Peter's passport had disappeared. I was now carrying someone with no proof of identity or legal entry into Algeria. This was rapidly developing into a real crisis.

Now that the Land Rover was running again, my main priority was to get medical help for Peter. I took a main road, which in the desert was a wide sandy area covered with vehicle tyre tracks, and drove northwards towards In Salah as fast as I was able.

Eventually at a place called Arak I came to a large entrance to what seemed like a walled camp. In fact it turned out to be a military area, a fact which I'd failed to notice in my excitement on finding civilisation and potential help.

I leapt out the vehicle and rushed toward the guards who stood impassively on either side of two large metal gates. I had no Arabic to speak of so when I did come across a local, communications were limited. I remember pointing at Peter and shouting something like "Doctor, Doctor, this man is very sick".

I was shocked by the response. A torrent of words which meant nothing to me came from one of the guards. I didn't need a translator to understand the gist, we weren't welcome here! The other guard raised his AK47 to reinforce the point and I quickly decided that further attempts to ask for help would be futile.

Back in the vehicle I drove on for several hours until eventually reaching In Salah, a largish oasis town where I was confident I could find medical assistance. After making some enquiries I learned that there was indeed a medical clinic and I now had a difficult decision to make. Given the perilous state of affairs, Peter with no passport and no obvious means to pay for treatment, I realised that there could be serious consequences for me if asked to explain our circumstances. I might at the extreme be accused of assisting an illegal immigrant. Whilst I'm not proud of what I did next, my responsibilities were firstly to my wife and two young children in UK. I would be of no use to them languishing in an Algerian prison or being held pending payment of Peter's medical expenses.

Having found out where the medical centre was and what time they opened, I arrived some minutes before and laid Peter on the ground at the centre's entrance before driving off. I was gambling on the medical staff taking him in and caring for him before any issues of passport and money arose.

I was later to learn that he was suffering from dehydration. In addition he had sunstroke and malaria, compounded by the effects of bilharzia, a waterborne disease which he had likely contracted from Lake Tanganyika. The medical centre had undoubtedly saved his life, he'd received help just in time, but what was I to do now?

UK Government to the Rescue

With Peter in safe hands I pondered my situation. What money I had would just about get me back to England. If I returned to the centre I faced the prospect of being asked to pay and also potential unwelcome police involvement. As a fellow traveller of someone who had no visible proof of legal entry into Algeria, I felt there would definitely be serious consequences. What was I to do?

As I was in a largish town with a post office I managed to book an international telephone call to my wife in England. I hurriedly explained my predicament and as usual she proposed a sensible solution. Whilst living in Lusaka we had become good friends with several of the British High Commission staff there. She suggested that she could contact one of them, James, and see if he could precipitate some action. Having passed on details of where Peter was, I hung up, feeling both grateful for my wife's support and more than a little homesick. I was hugely relieved that I was no longer responsible for Peter's welfare, as selfish as this may seem, I was grateful that his welfare was in others' hands and I could now continue my journey alone.

I wasn't party to the details of who James spoke to, or what strings, if any, were pulled, but thankfully Peter did recover and was eventually returned to the UK. We were to have one final conversation several weeks after I'd finally returned home.

Westwards to Reggane

Now that I was a free agent, no longer responsible for my passenger, I was finally able to relax. I felt a new sense of freedom and renewed excitement at the prospect of what lay ahead. Leaving In Salah there was a passable road northwards to Morocco where I planned to meet up with my wife. She would fly to Agadir and we'd complete the final 6 weeks of the journey together.

I'd met a Swedish chap on the way to Tamanrasset who was driving an old diesel land rover with even less horsepower than mine. I'd christened him the 'mad Swede' in my notes from the journey, probably because he seemed to have scant regard for any kind of plan and would go pretty much anywhere his old bus would take him. We'd met up again at In Salah, over 600 kms north of Tamanrasset. His enthusiasm and sense of adventure must have rubbed off on me. Instead of continuing on the main track north which would have been the sensible thing to do given the road conditions of the time, I decided to veer off. I'd noticed a place on my Michelin map called Reggane, almost directly due West of In Salah. From there it looked like a more direct route to the border crossing with Morocco that I was heading for. The Swede assured me there was a serviceable track and so with my trusty Silva compass and Boy Scout navigation skills, I set off alone. With hindsight, this could so easily have been the end of my journey.

The track seemed passable; vehicles had definitely been here before me. My own vehicle left fresh shallow tracks in the sand which I was later to be thankful for. I carried on for the best part of 70 miles. I'd seen little of interest so far, no signs of life, no dwellings, vehicles, camels, wildlife, nothing. Undeterred, I carried on westwards. I calculated another 70 miles or so and I should be approaching Reggane. After a couple more hours the tracks I'd been following simply disappeared. There were no signs that any vehicles had been along here previously. I felt an unease and wondered where I'd missed the track. I searched around and saw what might be a slight detour. A track seemed to go down the side of a steep slope. At the bottom surely the track would carry on I thought.

Gingerly I pointed my Land Rover straight down the slope. After a hundred yards or so the way got considerably steeper and the sand softer and deeper. Progress was slow and finally I ground to a halt. To go any further could be dangerous. On foot now I headed down to the bottom of the slope to explore.

What I found alarmed me. Nothing. No road, no vehicle tracks, just sand, certainly no signs of any route westwards.

Foolishly I'd committed myself to a course of action without fully thinking it through. In that moment I decided that I'd go no further. I'd give up on my plan to visit Reggane and I'd retrace my steps, going back to where I'd started from all those hours ago. I'd then take the main road north.

This left me with the not inconsiderable problem of how to turn around on the steep sandy slope and get back up to the top.

I carefully started to turn the Land Rover around, reckoning that reversing back up the slope would be too difficult. I was concerned that I'd roll over given the severe angle of the slope but after several minutes ANA45 was facing the correct way. Using the lowest gear I had, I gently released the clutch. The drive train juddered, wheels turned, but only to dig into the soft sand. I extracted my multipurpose spade, an impressive looking item that was more suited to latrine duty than shifting large quantities of sand. However it was all I had and would have to do. I set to, digging the 4 wheels free as best I could, an exhausting process in the intense heat of the day. Back in the vehicle I tried again to get some momentum. Once again I sank into the soft sand. I realised I'd need extra assistance if I was to negotiate the slope successfully.

Strapped to the side of the Land Rover I had two old original army steel sand ladders. These were heavy but designed to provide that extra traction needed to get going when bogged down. Using them was a laborious process. Dig down in front of each rear wheel, jam in the sand ladders, take off for as far as you could go before bogging down again, then repeat the whole process. In my case, progress was limited to the length of the sand ladder, some 5 feet. My journey to the top was completed therefore in 5 foot increments, and each time I set off the clutch juddered and the gearbox complained at the brutal load placed on them. I was seriously worried now; if the clutch went I'd be stranded alone away from any possibility of rescue. It was a huge physical effort in the harsh heat of the day and with hindsight I should have waited until first light the following morning to attempt this. By then the sand and conditions would be at their coolest.

A couple of hours later I reached the top genuinely feeling that I'd cheated death. This may sound overly dramatic but that was how I felt at the time. I spent the night at the top of the hill, both exhausted and elated.

Waking early the following morning all I had to do now was follow my original tracks back the 200 odd kilometres I'd come the previous day. Suffice to say that was the only advice I took from the mad Swede, we never met up again, probably just as well!

L: The 'Mad Swede'.

This gorge was nearly to prove my downfall.

Digging myself out.

Holed Below the Waterline!

I was enjoying my new found freedom now that I was alone in ANA45. I bounced across the Saharan sands, with Mick Jagger's *'She's the Boss'* album playing full volume on my trusty cassette car radio, encouraging me to go faster.

The 70's had produced so many fabulous rock bands and albums which were perfect to keep you awake when driving long distances. My favourite tracks included Golden Earing's 'Radar Love': *It's my baby callin', sayin', "I need you here" And it's a half past four and I'm shiftin' gear...*, anything from the legend Carlos Santana, and of course the iconic Thin Lizzy with Phil Lynott on bass and my favourite guitarist Gary Moore on lead guitar. Sadly Phil had died in January of 1986, he was only 4 years older than I was.

I'm not sure exactly when I tuned in to a new sensation whilst driving. We Land Rover owners are constantly alert to any new noises or resonances. They usually herald potential trouble and almost certainly involve time and expense to rectify. This latest sign was not so much a new noise, but a strange kind of disassociation between my seat, the steering wheel and the dashboard. It was difficult to pinpoint exactly what was going on. Whenever I crashed into a dip in the sandy track and rose out of it, it felt as if the rear of the Land Rover and I were going in different directions. I could swear that the dashboard was flexing, like a deep sea container ship crashing over huge Atlantic waves.

As I was in the Sahara this made no sense! Perhaps another warm beer would help. The desert tracks were long but well defined by now. I was on a clear heading to Figuig, the border post into Morocco. All my focus was on a smooth entry into what would be I hoped a relatively westernised country in comparison to where I'd come from.

I'd arranged to meet my wife in Agadir for a grand reunion. By chance, her brother and sister in law had also planned a holiday there at the same time. We'd arranged to spend one night in the same hotel that they would be staying in to catch up. Bearing in mind that one night in this hotel would cost as much as I'd been spending on several weeks travel it would then be camping all the way back home!

Arriving at Figuig I found that once again I was persona non grata. To all intents and purposes I was not going to be permitted to enter Morocco here. Having come so far I felt intensely frustrated. A heated discussion ensued with the border officials. They 'suggested' I drive to Oujda, another border post nearly 400 kms north, and putting me further away from Agadir. I reluctantly had to accept that this was the only way I was going to get out of Algeria and into Morocco.

The main road in Algeria.

Heading North to Oujda, I began to feel that ANA45 was somehow not as she should be. The dashboard was definitely flexing, seemingly independently to the rest of the vehicle.

I stopped and crawled underneath. To my horror I discovered the cause of this strange movement. The indestructible box ladder chassis with no rust whatsoever (having spent its entire life in

37

Africa), was holed below the waterline! Only the bottom section of the box was still intact on either side. Three of the four sides had split completely. There was a large gap and the entire chassis was flexing up and down around the remaining surface of the frame.

The weight of the vehicle, including my huge extra fuel tank and roof rack loaded with all those jerry cans, had proved too much for the chassis. I had visions of the last intact section giving way as well and ANA45 sinking gracefully into the desert sand. This was not good. If this happened I would quite possibly miss the reunion with my wife and in-laws. In the worst case scenario I wouldn't even make it to Oujda, stranded on route. Word would be out around the bars in Lusaka, Robert sank without trace in Algeria, never to be seen again!

So I did what any intrepid traveller would have done, turned up the volume on my cassette radio and carried on. I wondered if a leaf falling in Ho Chi Minh city had something to do with this chaos!

Broken Chassis.

The Reunion and Repairs

I arrived at Oujda with no further incident and thankfully was permitted entry to Morocco. Some three days later I was in Agadir and managed to be on time to meet my wife's flight from London. It was an emotional reunion. I had lost nearly 3 stones in weight and was barely recognisable from when I'd left Lusaka. My wife had also lost weight. She had had to reintegrate into life in Kent with two children under the age of two, on her own. This would have been difficult enough had I been there as well, but on her own had surely been a real challenge.

However we were determined to make the most of the remaining journey and celebrated with my in-laws that evening in their hotel. I remember demolishing a huge plate of seafood which unfortunately all came back up later. I simply wasn't used to eating so much rich protein after nearly 5 months existing on vegetables and rice.

The next day I explained that we had to get ANA45 some urgent attention. The chassis needed strengthening which would involve welding. I anticipated a major bill. The petrol tank would have to be removed to gain access safely and it looked like the job could take at least a day.

How naive I was! Word got out that I was looking for a reliable garage. A man appeared and guided us to the side of the road. He said he was the man for the job. Surely he wasn't intending to fix the chassis here. I'd had visions of a 4-post vehicle lift operated by a professional mechanic in overalls.

Minutes later he'd covered the petrol tank with hessian sacks soaked in water. Then a welding machine appeared and before we knew it clouds of sparks were being generated directly next to the fuel tank. I assured my wife this was fine, whilst secretly terrified that a huge explosion was imminent. I think I suggested we went off for a camel ride to distract from this. In any event a repair was quickly completed to both sides of the chassis and ANA45 subsequently sailed through an MOT on return to England.

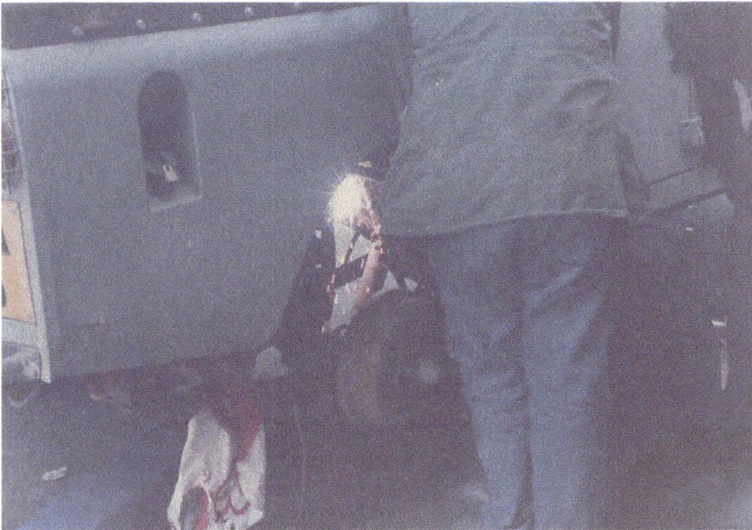

Welding the chassis in the street.

In The Doghouse?

Some time had passed since picking up my wife from the airport at Agadir. Camel rides had been experienced. The Atlas mountains traversed. Delicious sardines eaten on the beach at Essaouira. Fez's famous Chouara tannery explored and smell endured. Marrakesh's souk navigated and the odd Moroccan rug purchased for good measure. In short the time had now come to leave Morocco and head home through Spain.

By now I'd become blasé about border crossings. I'd experienced all types, both efficient, slow, and in Cameroon, closed completely for the afternoon due to the football fever! This one however was different. I had no idea how the Spanish border officials would react to ANA45 who by now was looking severely battle scarred and also to me in my very tatty shorts, flip-flops and rampant beard after several months' neglect. In short the journey had taken its toll on my appearance. I said little of these concerns to my wife as we arrived at the border. After all I was the experienced one here.

Then my worst nightmare happened. In my mind it was Midnight Express all over again some eight years after the film had first shocked cinema audiences. I would spend my days in a derelict prison devoid of any creature comforts. My wife would be dragged into a horrific legal battle to establish her innocence. In short disaster on an epic scale was imminent. All these thoughts swirled around my head when to my horror a Spanish Immigration and Customs official appeared with an enormous Alsatian sniffer dog.

Trained to identify illegal substances from a young age, rewarded for finding even the remotest lingering scent of any number of illegal drugs, this animal, to whom no amount of denial would make the slightest difference, was about to leap into the bowels of my Land Rover.

I turned pale, my heart rate increased rapidly. What, if anything, should I say to my wife to prewarn her that we might both be dragged away unceremoniously for drug smuggling? Explaining to the Spanish officials that anything found tucked away into the innermost crevices of ANA45 actually belonged to a since departed fellow passenger (address and whereabouts unknown, no passport, many medical issues etc.) would of course be treated with incredulity. In fact I didn't even believe the story myself, it sounded so implausible.

The next couple of minutes were to be the longest in my life thus far. The Alsatian leapt into ANA45 and proceeded to sniff methodically for any scent that would bring it reward from its handler. Like a sommelier nosing a fine 1929 Chateau Petrus, it was taking its job most seriously.

"OK, you may go now" said the official. I was bemused. *"You can go now"* he repeated. We were free to enter Spain. No prison sentence, I could hardly believe it. My wife must have thought I was just relieved and emotional to have completed the final crossing into Europe. I made no attempt to explain further, some things were better left unsaid!

Breakdown on Boulevard Périphérique

We had driven up the Spanish coast alongside the Mediterranean. From Gibraltar to Malaga and on to Alicante. The coastline was one huge building site, tall cranes dominated the skyline and high rise buildings were springing up everywhere, the construction industry was obviously the one to be in. The other business which seemed to be booming judging by the number of signs displayed was private investigation. 'Investigador privado' signs were all around. I wondered naively if this had anything to do with British expats fleeing justice in the UK, or husbands and wives looking to confirm their suspicions.

Soon we were in France and our route to Calais took us via Paris. It was a weekday and somehow we found ourselves gridlocked on the Périphérique, the French equivalent to what would be called the M25 around London. The Land Rover was a nightmare to drive in stop start conditions and progress was pitifully slow. Priority seemed to be given to vehicles entering the ring road from the right and with no obvious hard shoulder for breakdowns it was all very confusing and stressful.

It was about to become a whole lot more stressful. The engine misfired and stopped completely. We were stranded amongst impatient Parisian workers on route to their offices and factories and now we were causing a huge logjam. I can remember thinking that it was a stroke of luck that our number plate wasn't British and that we weren't displaying a GB sticker. That would surely have made matters even worse!

Bonnet up I investigated the cause of the problem. Deep down I already knew what it would be. Chaos theory or not, the fault was with that old distributor which had finally given up. With less than 250 miles to go we were stranded on one of the busiest ring roads in Europe and I'd given my spare distributor to Ahmed in Algeria!

No choice but to effect a temporary repair and limp to a Land Rover agent for spares. I think we managed to get going again with some minor parts from the garage and made it back to Customs and Immigration at Dover without further incident. I'd anticipated a long discussion here but in the final event it was all very straightforward. The customs officials were extremely helpful and explained what I needed to do to import ANA45 into the UK.

And so our trip came to a close. Six months had gone by in a flash. We were now home.

Parting of the Ways

After arriving back in the UK, ANA45 had acquired a new identity. From memory she was now on an M registration plate, the year of original manufacture being 1973. An MOT had been required. She had no windscreen washers, for some reason these had never been fitted. She needed brakes that actually stopped within the required distance. In fact she needed quite a few extras to meet the MOT requirements of the day.

What she didn't need was any welding. Even though she was 13 years old and had spent many thousands of kilometres off road there was absolutely no rust to be found anywhere. Her chassis, resplendent with the thick steel reinforcing plates that the Moroccan welder had added whilst on the side of the road in Agadir, was as sound as the day she'd first left the factory.

I was slowly settling back into life in the UK. This involved circulating my CV to potential employers. I was confident of getting a good job quickly. Unfortunately this wasn't to be the case. My experience in Zambia wasn't particularly well received by the personnel managers of the day. Certainly my 6 months' journey home was regarded more as a hindrance than a demonstration of my problem solving skills and self motivation. Things were looking bleak. Bills had to be paid. I had to get employment.

Through a friend who was going out with a tree surgeon, I managed to get a temporary job in his tree surgery business. I figured that this would keep me going whilst I tried to regain a foothold back into white collar employment in England.

Due to the nature of his business the jobs often took me into different rural locations in Kent, often off road. My Land Rover was ideal for this. I would confidently be able to get on site whatever the weather or ground conditions.

I stayed with Adrian for 6 months. During this time I learnt all manner of tree surgery skills. One of these was how to thin a pine forest. This included a process called snedding. First cutting the tree down. Then removing the side branches from the trunk, picking it up at the base and running as fast as possible out of the wood whilst dragging it behind you. Having sat in a vehicle for the previous six months you can imagine that I was less than totally effective at this manoeuvre, though I did improve over time!

Anyway, I digress. The point here was that ANA45, as was, was costing me almost 50% of my daily wage in running costs. This was clearly unsustainable. The time had sadly come to admit that a 4x4, however good on the one week of the year of snow that Kent experienced, was simply not a sensible vehicle to own as a daily driver.

I advertised in the local paper and the next day an interested party arrived to look her over. He was somewhat bemused by the enormous fuel tank, which had been empty now for several months. Now it was even more of a death trap than when originally full, due to all the fuel vapour. I suspect that he'd calculated its value in scrap metal and this made the deal even sweeter for him. I think the sum of £825 was agreed, cash exchanged and he prepared to drive off.

I took a final look at her, my pride and joy for the previous 5 years. Every inch of her brought back memories. The wrinkles in the front passenger wing where one of President Kenneth Kaunda's outriders had impaled his motorcycle as he sailed gracefully over the bonnet and landed unceremoniously in a heap on the road. Thankfully he survived though I had spent an anxious few days wondering if I was to be prosecuted or worse for entering Independence

Avenue on a green light! I should have known that Presidential cavalcades in Africa don't stop at red lights!

My final gaze fell upon the passenger door handle. I smiled at the memory of what I shall call the 'Chachacha road incident'. Chachacha road runs parallel to the main Cairo road in Lusaka's city centre and in those days was not commonly frequented by expats for security reasons. It was quite rundown and mainly home to small shops selling coca cola and small domestic and hardware items. The white population mainly stuck to Cairo road for shopping and banking when in town.

I can't recall what required me to stop here temporarily. Presumably I'd stopped off at a shop to purchase something before carrying on to my destination, a private medical centre nearby. Coming out of the shop I noticed immediately that things weren't as I'd left them. The passenger door was ajar, the handle and lock had been forced and the brown paper bag which I'd left on the passenger seat was gone.

I wish I'd seen the look on the perpetrator's face when they opened the package. The bag contained stool samples from my wife and I to be delivered to the medical centre for a routine check! It was almost worth the expense of a new door handle and lock as I dined out on this story for months afterwards!

But the time had finally come to say goodbye to ANA45. My home for the last 6 months, she'd transported me almost uneventfully across at least twelve African countries, become part of the family, but always a drain on my bank account! As she departed off down the road I wondered if I'd ever be able to own another Land Rover. Maybe there was something to this chaos theory after all!

Postscript Some weeks after arriving back in UK I received a phone call from Peter. He's calling to thank us for arranging his safe return to the UK I thought. Our conversation was brief. He wanted to know where his cooking equipment was that had been in the Land Rover when I'd left him in Algeria...

The author in the Sahara.

A peaceful place to camp in the Sahara.

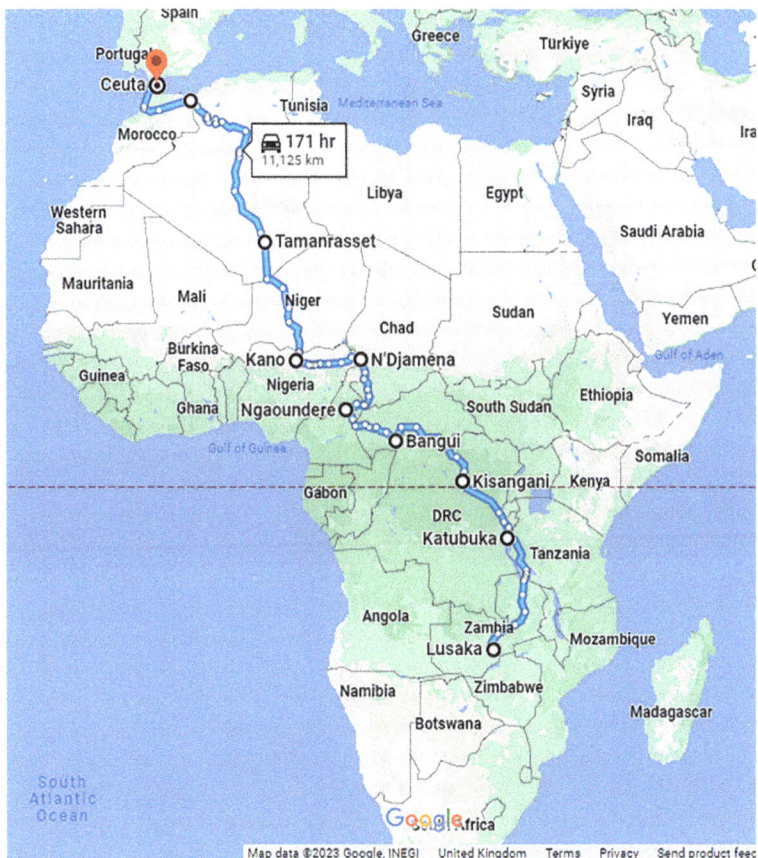

www.ingramcontent.com/pod-product-compliance
Lightning Source LLC
Chambersburg PA
CBHW040122070426
42448CB00043B/3481